ABOUT THE AUTHOR

Robert Gardiner lives in Australia and was born in the goldfields town of Ballarat in Victoria.
He studied Graphic Design in Bendigo before moving to Melbourne 20 years ago to
work as a Finished Artist for some of the best Graphic Designers in Australia.
He still lives in Melbourne with his wife Angela and their two children,
some of whom still refuse to colour within the lines.

DEDICATION

For my two happy little scribblers, Elise and Lucas.

THE SUPERCAR Colouring Book

Robert Gardiner

AUSTIN MACAULEY
PUBLISHERS LTD.

Copyright © Robert Gardiner (2016)

The right of Robert Gardiner to be identified as author of this work has been asserted by his in accordance with section 77 and 78 of the Copyright, Designs and Patents Act 1988.

All rights reserved. No part of this publication may be reproduced, stored in a retrieval system, or transmitted in any form or by any means, electronic, mechanical, photocopying, recording, or otherwise, without the prior permission of the publishers.

Any person who commits any unauthorized act in relation to this publication may be liable to criminal prosecution and civil claims for damages.

A CIP catalogue record for this title is available from the British Library.

ISBN 9781786293800 (Paperback)
ISBN 9781786293817 (Hardback)
ISBN 9781786293824 (eBook)

www.austinmacauley.com

First Published (2016)
Austin Macauley Publishers Ltd.
25 Canada Square
Canary Wharf
London
E14 5LQ

1929 Ford Coupé - Hot Rod

1939 Auto Union Type D

1954 Mercedes Benz 300 SL Coupé

1955 Maserati 250S

1963 Jaguar E-Type Coupé

1964 Ferrari 250 GTO

1965 Aston Martin DB5

1968 Ford GT40

1968 Shelby Cobra 427

1969 Ford Mustang Boss 429

1970 Corvette Stingray

1970 Pontiac Firebird 350

1970 Porsche LeMans

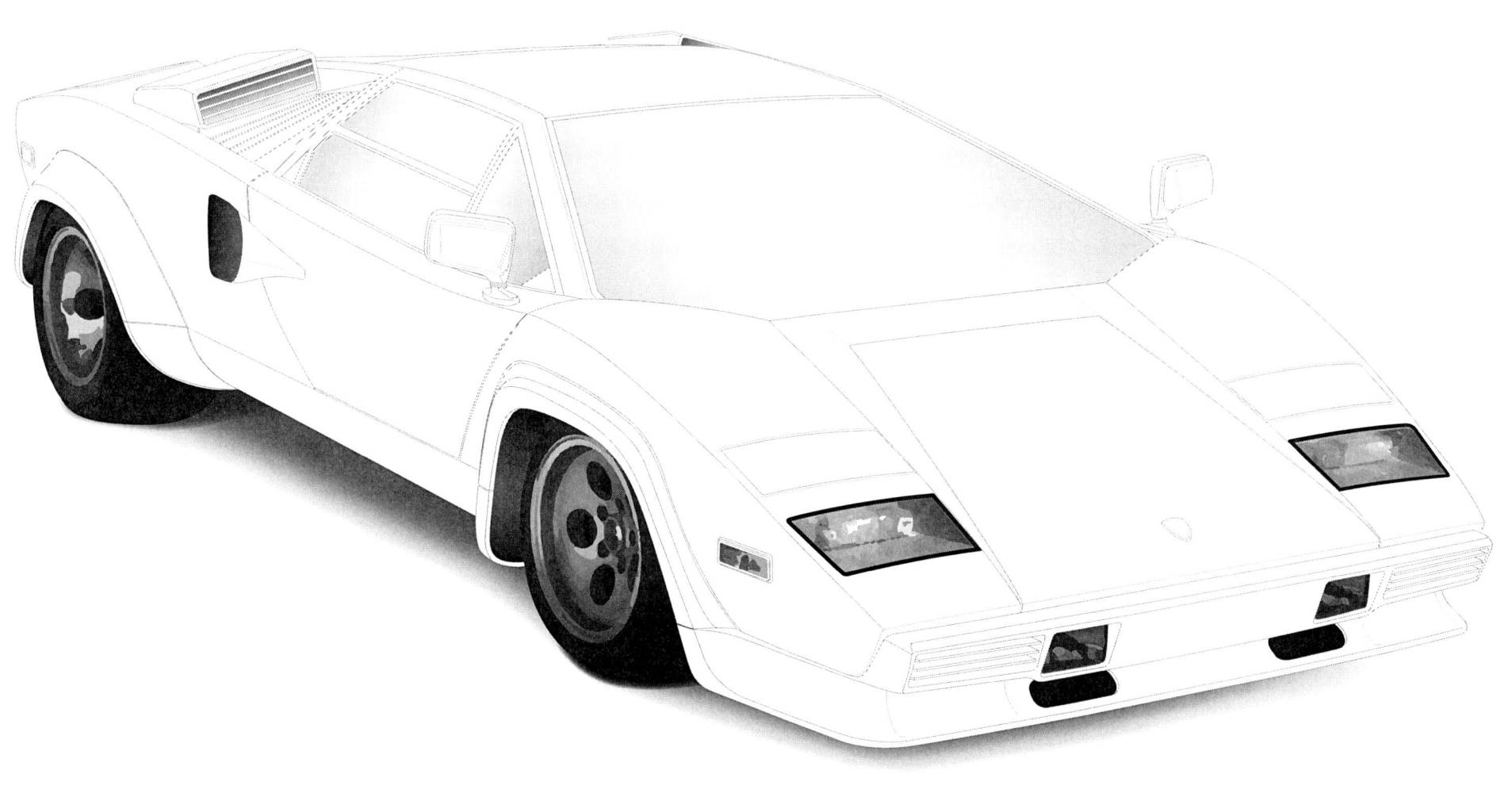

1980 Lamborghini Countach

1999 Nissan Skyline GTR R34

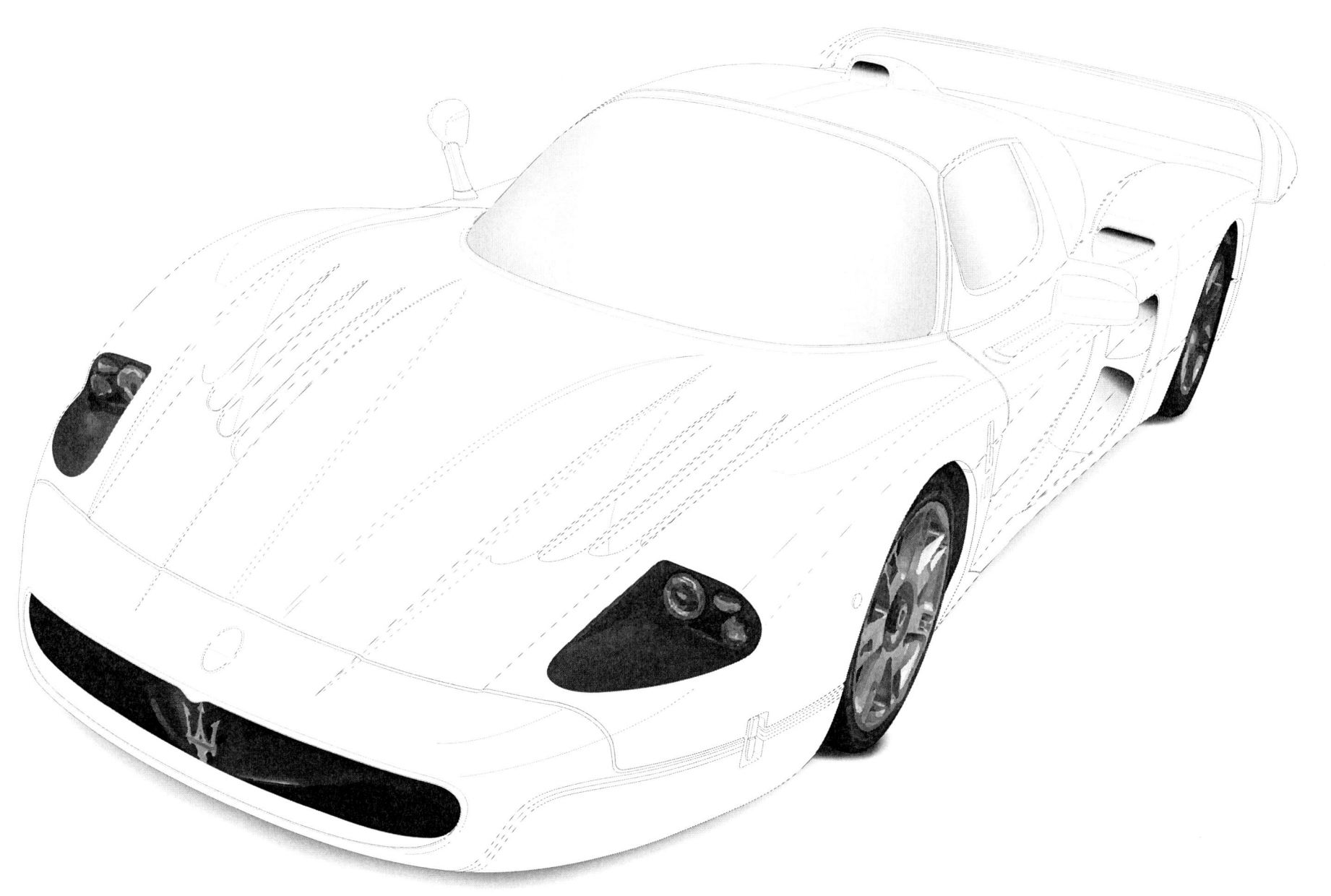

2005 Maserati MC12

2008 BMW M1 Hommage

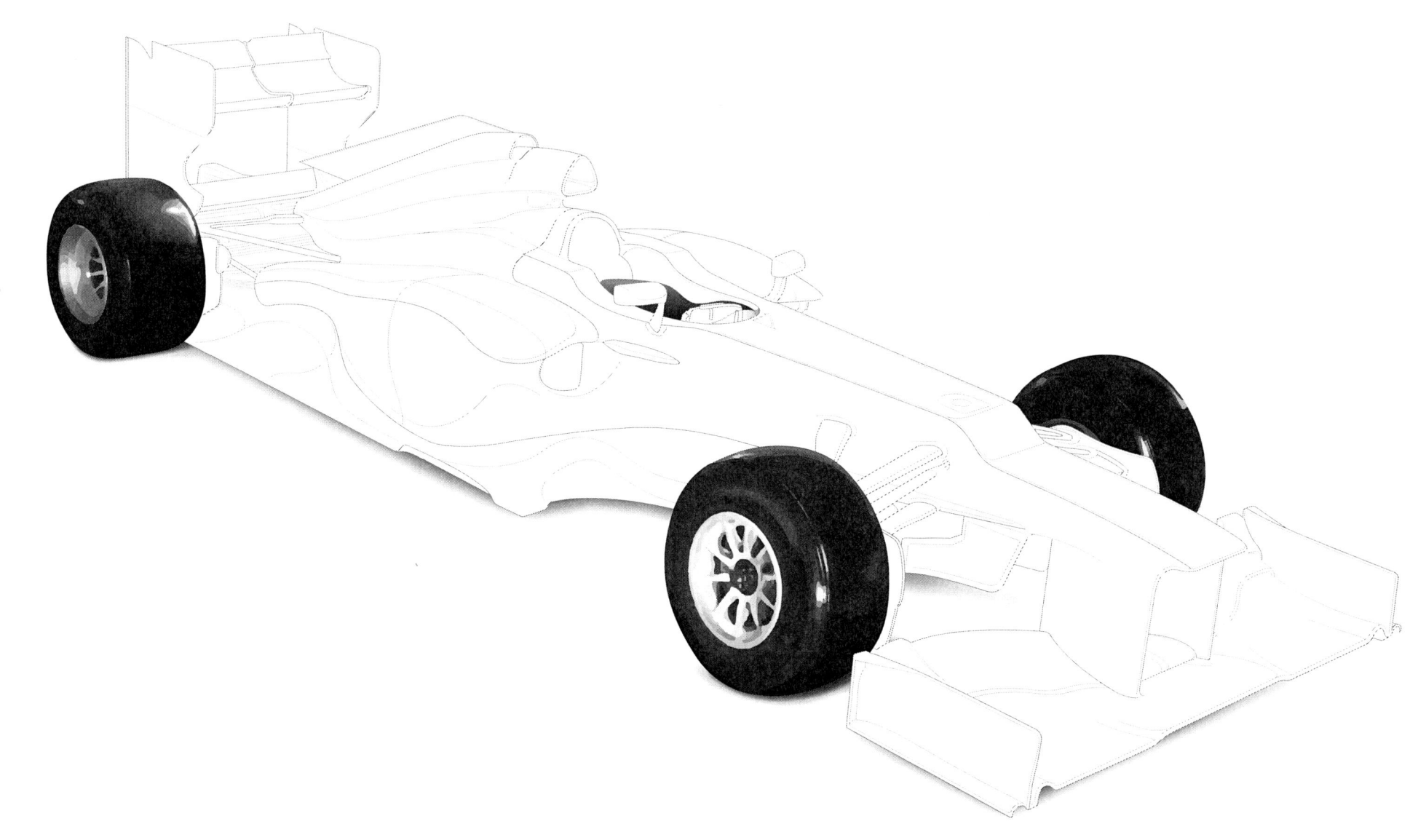

2012 Ferrari Formula 1

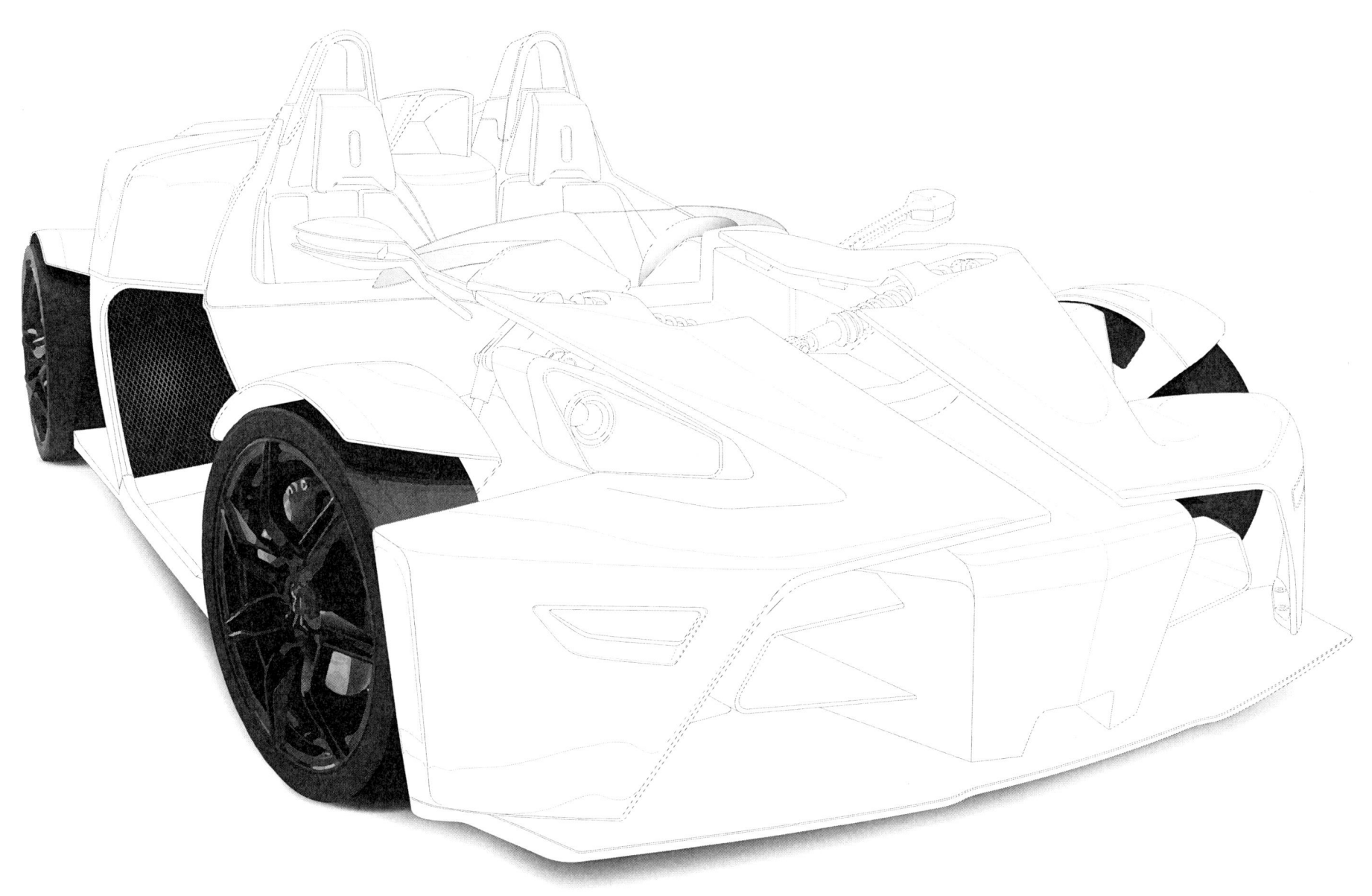

2012 KTM X-Bow

2012 Lamborghini Aventador

2012 Lotus Exige

2012 Pagani Huayra

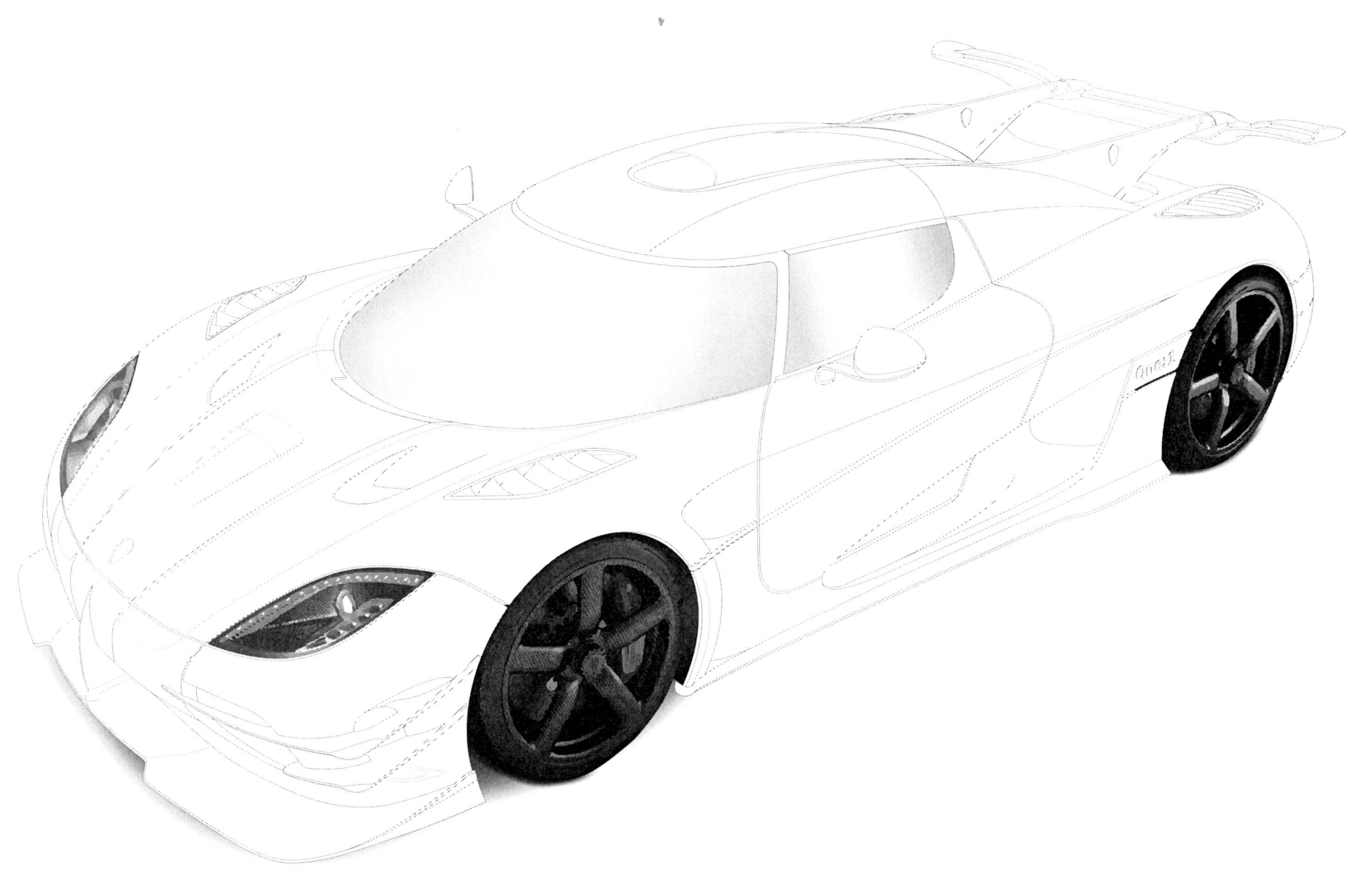

2014 Koenigsegg One:1

2014 LaFerrari F150

2015 Aston Martin DB10

2015 Bugatti GT

2015 Dodge Challenger

2015 LaFerrari Hybrid Concept

2015 McLaren P1 GTR

2016 Mercedes Benz VGT